Nonfiction Reading Comprehension

This book belongs to

....

Lyn Jones

Contents

Great White Sharks 4

The Sahara Desert.......................6

Dogs That Help Us 8

The Trojan Horse 10

Lock It In...................................... 12

Hunting Buffalo 14

Clues in Rocks 16

Measuring Weather.....................18

Gods and Goddesses...................20

Popular Penguins 22

Living In Tepees 24

Fantastic Fossils 26

American Black Bears...............28

What Is a Pyramid? 30

Spots and Stripes 32

Dinosaur Puzzles 34

Tomb Painting.......................36

Underwater Treasure.................38

Asian Bears 40

Bashful Bats.................................42

Underwater Food Chain 44

Our Brain 46

Helpful Huskies 48

The Clean Machine.........................50

Kinds of Rocks.............................52

Life in the Spinifex.......................54

Heavenly Colors.........................56

Super Swingers............................58

In the Trees.................................60

The Roman Army.......................62

Eating Food 64

Chapters of History....................66

Answers 68

Great White Sharks

Read the story about great white sharks.
If you find a new word, look at the words
around it to help work out the meaning.

Sharks are fish. All sharks have a tail and fins.
Great whites are scary sharks. They are large with
sharp teeth and powerful jaws. They feed on fish and
seals. Sometimes a great white may attack a swimmer
because the swimmer may look like a seal.

1 Answer these questions about the story.

(a) What do all sharks have?

....

(b) What does the great white feed on?

....

(c) Look at the picture. What things make a swimmer
    look like a seal?

....

2 Write the word in the story that is the opposite to:

(a) blunt .... (b) small ....

(c) weak ....

3 Here's a fun crossword. The answers are words in the story.

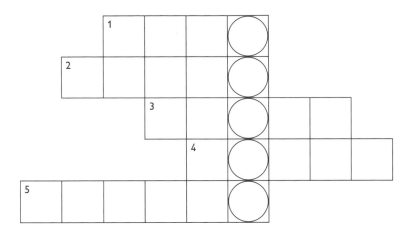

1. A shark has powerful ....

2. A great white has sharp ....

3. Great whites feed on fish, ... , dolphins, and turtles.

4. .... whites are scary sharks.

5. Sometimes a great white may .... a swimmer.

4 Write down each letter in the circles of the puzzle.

What is the mystery word? ....

☆☆ Whale sharks are as big as a bus.

The Sahara Desert

Here is some information about the Sahara Desert. Read the story and then enjoy completing the fun activities.

The Sahara is the largest desert in the world. It stretches across northern Africa. People who live in the Sahara wear special clothes to keep cool. They use camels to cross the desert. Camels can live in the desert. They can go for many days with little food and water.

1   Are these sentences True or False?
    Color in the star next to the correct answer.

(a) The Sahara is small.
    ☆ True   ☆ False

(b) The Sahara is in Africa.
    ☆ True   ☆ False

(c) People use camels to travel in the Sahara.
    ☆ True   ☆ False

(d) Camels must eat every day.
    ☆ True   ☆ False

(e) It is very hot in the desert.
    ☆ True   ☆ False

2 Look at the picture. It is very hot, dry, and windy in the desert. People cover their head, nose, and mouth. Can you say why?

....

3 Cross out every second letter in each line to discover the secret message.

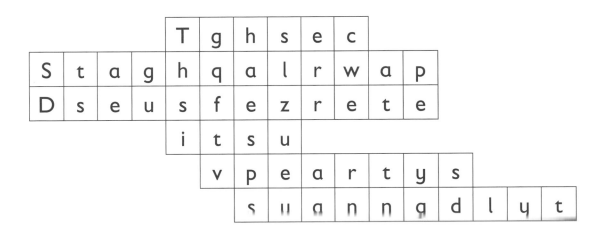

		T	g	h	s	e	c		
S	t	a	g	h	q	a	l	r	w	a	p
D	s	e	u	s	f	e	z	r	e	t	e
		i	t	s	u				
		v	p	e	a	r	t	y	s
			s	u	a	n	n	g	d	l	y	t

The message is

....

Dogs That Help Us

Read the story about dogs that help us. Complete the fun activities when you finish reading the story.

Great Danes were once used as hunting dogs. They are very large, gentle dogs. Search dogs are trained to help find people who are lost or trapped after a disaster. Cattle dogs are working dogs, too. Their main job is to keep cattle moving in the right direction.

1   Choose which dog from the story fits the description.

(a) I belong with a rescue worker.   ....

(b) I belong with a hunter.   ....

(c) I belong with a farmer.   ....

(d) I am a large dog.   ....

(e) I can find lost people.   ....

(f) I tell cattle what to do.   ....

2 Read each description and then guess the word.
   Each answer rhymes with the word "dog."

   (a) It croaks.   ....

   (b) It is a part of a dead tree. ....

   (c) It looks like mist.   ....

   (d) to run   ....

3 Help the cattle dog find the lost cow.

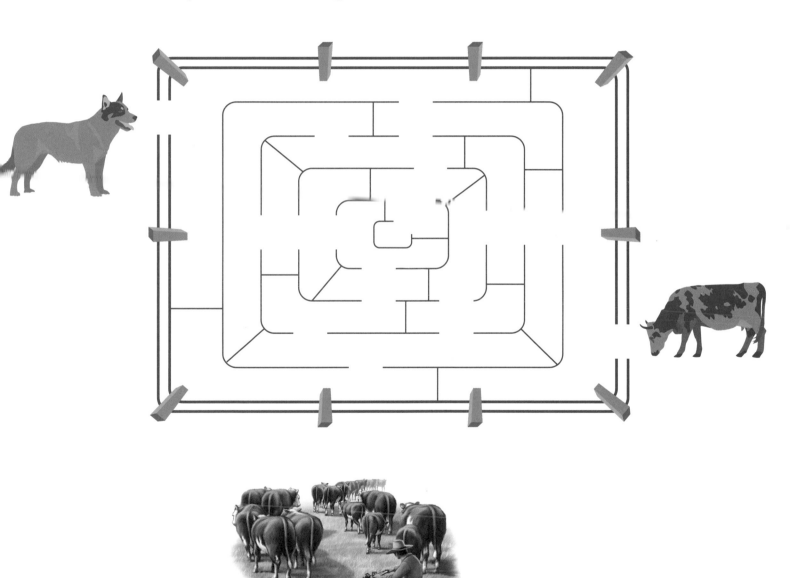

The Trojan Horse

Let's find out about the story of the Trojan horse. Complete the fun activities when you finish reading the story.

The Greek king Odysseus wanted to own the city of Troy, but the city wall kept him out. So crafty Odysseus hid soldiers inside a huge, hollow, wooden horse. He gave it to the Trojans as a gift. They took it inside the city walls. When it was inside, the Greek soldiers jumped out and won the war.

1 Read these questions about the story, then color in the star next to the correct answer.

(a) What city did Odysseus want to own?
☆ Rome   ☆ Greece   ☆ Troy

(b) Where did the Greek soldiers hide?
☆ behind the wall   ☆ inside the wooden horse
☆ in the city buildings

(c) What stopped Odysseus from getting inside the city?
☆ the city wall   ☆ he was scared of the Trojans
☆ the wooden horse

2 Number these sentences in the correct order.

.... The wooden horse was left outside the city of Troy.

.... Greek soldiers hid in the wooden horse.

.... The Greek soldiers jumped out of the horse.

.... The Trojans took the wooden horse inside the city.

.... Odysseus built a wooden horse.

3 Draw a line from each word to match
it with its meaning.

crafty   empty

gift   clever

wooden   made of wood

hollow   very big

huge   present

Lock It In

Let's find out how a lock and key work. Use a dictionary to find the meaning of new words, then try the word puzzles.

When a key is put into a lock, it makes a row of tiny metal pins move. With the right key, the row of pins will line up straight to open the lock. Keys lock and unlock doors. You need the right key to unlock a door.

1   Number these sentences in the correct order.

.... The row of tiny pins moves.

.... The row of tiny pins lines up straight.

.... The key goes into the lock.

.... The lock opens.

2   Circle words that rhyme with "key."

see	they	she	be
keen	sea	free	blue

3 Look at the words in the box and choose the ones that go with the words below.

saucer   key   pepper   fork   socks   chair

(a) lock and   ....   (d) shoes and   ....

(b) salt and   ....   (e) knife and   ....

(c) cup and   ....   (f) table and   ....

4 Work through the maze to see which key opens the lock.

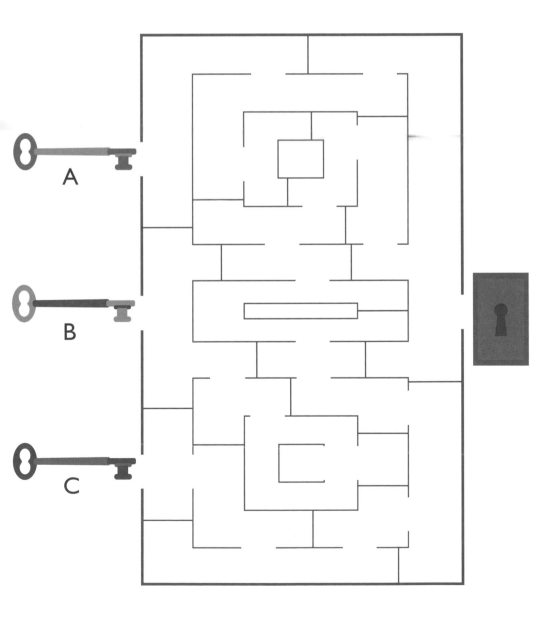

Hunting Buffalo

Read the story about hunting buffalo. If you find a new word, look at the words around it to help work out the meaning.

In North America, lands that are flat with no hills are called the Plains. American Indians who lived on the Plains moved around on horses. They followed herds of buffalo and then killed them with spears and arrows. American Indians used buffalo skins for clothing, ate buffalo meat, and burned buffalo fat in lamps.

1   Color in the star next to the correct answer.

(a) In North America, land that is flat with
   no hills is called ....
   ☆ the Hills   ☆ the Flats   ☆ the Plains

(b) American Indians hunted for food on ....
   ☆ horses   ☆ buffalos   ☆ motorcycles

(c) Buffalo parts can be used
   for ....
   ☆ meat and spears
   ☆ meat and clothing
   ☆ clothing and arrows

A

2   Unscramble these letters to make words from the story.

aft   ....

sampl   ....

team   ....

shores   ....

3   Look closely at the picture.

Who said this?

Was it Indian (A) or Indian (B) or Buffalo (C)?

Help! Get out
of my way.

I have lots
of arrows to
help me hunt.

My spear is
sharp and my
horse is fast.

....

Clues in Rocks

Here is some information about rocks and fossils.
Read the story. Try to sound out new words.
Then enjoy completing the activities.

A fossil is part of an animal or plant that used to be alive, preserved in rock. Scientists dig into layers of rock to look for fossils. The fossil gives them a clue about animals that lived a long time ago. The scientists in the picture are digging out fossils of dinosaur bones.

1 Are these sentences True or False?
   Color in the star next to the correct answer.

   (a) Fossils help to tell us about animals from long ago.
      ☆ True   ☆ False

   (b) A fossil is part of something that used to be alive preserved in plastic.
      ☆ True   ☆ False

   (c) Fossils give a clue about animals that lived in zoos.
      ☆ True   ☆ False

   (d) A fossil is part of something that used to be alive preserved in rock.
      ☆ True   ☆ False

   (e) Scientists often find fossils in books.
      ☆ True   ☆ False

2 Find the words in the story that rhyme
   with these words.

   (a) book   ....

   (b) song   ....

   (c) phones   ....

3 Draw these "-ock" words in the box.

   r + ock =   l + ock =

   cl + ock =   s + ock =

Measuring Weather

What do you know about measuring weather? Read the story and then complete the activities to discover more about it.

Different places have different weather. You can measure the weather at home. Use a rain gauge to see how much rain falls each day. Use a thermometer to see how hot or cold the air is outside. Put it in the shade to protect it from the sun.

1 Read the story and then answer the questions.

(a) What is used to measure rain?

....

(b) What is used to measure how hot or cold the air is outside?

....

(c) Why do we keep a thermometer in the shade?

....

2 Think of a symbol to describe what these weather words mean and draw it in the boxes. One has been done for you.

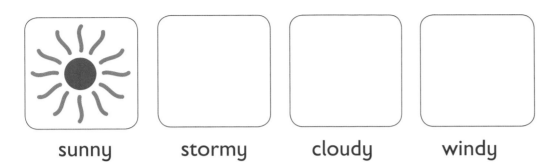

sunny   stormy   cloudy   windy

3 Find two clues in the picture that tell us that the weather is cool.

(a) ....

(b) ....

4 Search the word puzzle for the words in the list below and circle them.

CLOUD
COLD
FALL
GAUGE
HOT
RAIN
SPRING
SUMMER
SUN
THERMOMETER
WIND
WINTER

Gods and Goddesses

What do you know about ancient gods and goddesses? Read the story and use a dictionary to find the meaning of new words.

The ancient Romans prayed to many gods and goddesses. They killed animals as sacrifices to them and made special offerings of food and wine as gifts to the gods. Vesta was the Roman goddess of the fireplace. The picture shows women who kept a fire burning both day and night to honor Vesta.

1 Are these sentences True or False?
   Color in the star next to the correct answer.

   (a) The ancient Romans killed animals as
       sacrifices to the gods.
       ☆ True   ☆ False

   (b) The ancient Romans gave food and
       wine to the gods.
       ☆ True   ☆ False

   (c) The women put out the fire every night.
       ☆ True   ☆ False

2 Color in the star next to each correct answer.

   (a) What gifts were given to the gods?
       ☆ flowers   ☆ wine   ☆ food

   (b) Who was the Roman goddess of the fireplace?
       ☆ Zeus   ☆ Mars   ☆ Vesta

   (c) Look at the picture. What are the women doing?
       ☆ making spells   ☆ keeping a fire burning   ☆ making tea

3 Search the word puzzle for the names of these Greek and Roman
   gods and goddesses in the list below and circle them.

APHRODITE (goddess of love)   MARS (god of war)
APOLLO (god of the sun)   NIKE (goddess of victory)
ATHENA (goddess of wisdom)   POSEIDON (god of the sea)
HERA (queen of the gods)   VESTA (goddess of the hearth)
HERMES (messenger of the gods)   ZEUS (king of the gods)

```
            V  B  K  A  J
               V  M  T
               E  A  H
               S  R  E
         B  N  T  S  N  Z  A
      D  C  I  A  G  A  E  P  H
      M  P  K  V  Z  C  U  O  E
   C  J  H  E  R  M  E  S  L  R  R
   C  P  Q  C  G  N  B  M  L  A  A
   N  M  R  Y  D  Z  P  S  O  E  E
A  P  H  R  O  D  I  T  E  Q  O  Y  R
P  O  S  E  I  D  O  N  H  Z  Y  Q  X
```

Popular Penguins

Here is a story about penguins. Read the story and then have fun completing the activities.

Penguins are birds that cannot fly. They use their wings as flippers when they swim underwater. Penguins spend some of their life on land and some in the water. They live in the southern part of the world.

1 Are these sentences True or False?
   Color in the star next to the correct answer.

   (a) Penguins are birds.
      ☆ True   ☆ False

   (b) Penguins can fly.
      ☆ True   ☆ False

   (c) Penguins live in the northern part of the world.
      ☆ True   ☆ False

   (d) Penguins can swim underwater.
      ☆ True   ☆ False

2 Read the clues and match the penguin name to the drawing. Write your answers next to the correct penguin.

   I have black feet. I am an emperor penguin.

   I have a black stripe on my chest. I am a Magellanic penguin.

   I have a black line on my chin. I am a chinstrap penguin.

3 Fill in the no-clues crossword with these words.

PENGUIN
FLIPPERS
WATER
WORLD
SWIM

A..
....

yellow-eyed
penguin

fjordland
penguin

C..
....

B..
....

Living In Tepees

What do you know about American Indian tepees? Read the story and try the fun word puzzles.

American Indians lived right across North America long before people from Europe arrived. Indians on the Plains lived in tents called tepees. They were made from the skins of buffalo. People cooked food over a fireplace inside their tepee. The smoke went out through smoke flaps at the top.

1 Are these sentences True or False?
   Write your answer in the space provided.

(a) American Indians lived in North America
     before people from Europe arrived.   ....

(b) A dog is sleeping inside the tepee.   ....

(c) Only Indian girls have long hair.   ....

(d) Grandmother is cooking inside the tepee.   ....

2   Write the words in the story that rhyme
with these words.

(a) mood   ....

(b) song   ....

(c) joke   ....

(d) pop   ....

(e) wins   ....

3   Every column, row and mini-grid must contain
the letters of the key word "SKIN."

I			N
		S	
	I		
	K	I	

What is grandmother doing?

Fantastic Fossils

Let's learn some more about fossils. Read the story and then complete the fun activities.

Fossils can come from animals and plants. Animal bones left in the ground can turn into stone as time passes and become fossils. Fossils can also be made from plants. A leaf might fall into clay. The clay hardens and leaves an impression, or mark, in the shape of the plant. Some insects and fish have also become fossils.

plant fossil

1   Read the story and answer these questions.

(a) How does a bone become a fossil?

....

(b) As well as animal bones, what else can become a fossil?

....

2   Fill in the missing vowels in this sentence.

Vowels = a e i o u

Usu......lly, only th...... hard bony p......rts
of an......mals ar...... str......ng eno......gh
to m......ke f......ss......ls.

3 Here's a fun crossword. The answers are words in the story.

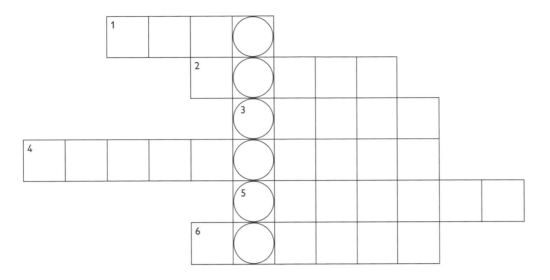

1. A .... might fall into clay.

2. Fossils are often made from animal ....

3. As time passes bones turn into ....

4. A mark left in the shape of something is called an ....

5. As well as dinosaurs, fish, and plants, ... can become fossils.

6. As well as dinosaurs, fish, and insects, ... can become fossils.

4 Write down each letter in the circles of the puzzle. What is the mystery word? ....

fish fossil

insect fossil

crab fossil

American Black Bears

Let's find out about American black bears. Use a dictionary to find the meaning of new words. Try the word puzzles, too.

There are eight different kinds of bears. Bears live in many places, but not in Africa, Australia, or Antarctica. American black bears have a thick, shaggy dark coat. They use their strong claws for tearing, digging, and climbing trees. Some American black bears are brown. American black bears live in the forests.

1 Read the story, then circle the correct answers to these questions.

(a) What are three ways an American black bear uses its claws?

tearing   flying   eating   digging   climbing

(b) What does "shaggy" mean?

untidy   smooth   dirty

(c) Where do American black bears live?

deserts   trees   forests

2   Are these sentences True or False?
    Color in the star next to the correct answer.

(a) An American black bear can climb trees.
    ☆ True   ☆ False

(b) An American black bear has a thick coat.
    ☆ True   ☆ False

(c) An American black bear is always black.
    ☆ True   ☆ False

3   Search the word puzzle for these 10 "bear" words.

ASIAN
BLACK
BROWN
CUB
GRIZZLY
PANDA
POLAR
SLOTH
SPECTACLED
SUN

```
                A
              B S S
            G R P O I
          B R O E L P A
        C L I W C S O U N
      Z U A Z N T L L S I A
        B C Z U A O A U D
          K L P C T R N
            Y Q L H A
              W E P
                D
```

American black bears

What Is a Pyramid?

Read the story about pyramids. Use a dictionary to find the meaning of new words then have fun completing the activities.

A pyramid has sides that are shaped like triangles. The sides meet at the top. Inside are chambers, passageways, and shafts. Long ago, people made pyramids from brick or stone. They took many years to build. Inside the pyramids in Egypt are the tombs of dead kings and queens.

1 Help the Egyptians build the homophone pyramid with these homophone stones. Homophones are words that have the same sound, like "to" and "two."

1. a homophone for "buy"

2. a homophone for "sun"

3. a homophone for "no"

4. a homophone for "ate"

5. a homophone for "build"

2 Match the jigsaw parts to make a sentence.
   Color the parts that make one sentence the same color.

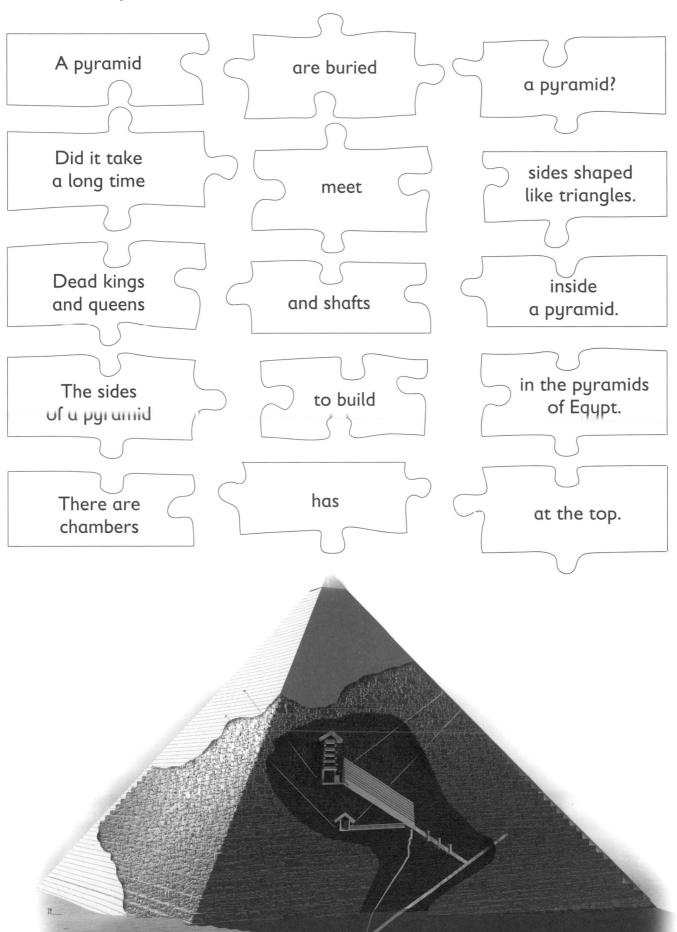

A pyramid

are buried

a pyramid?

Did it take
a long time

meet

sides shaped
like triangles.

Dead kings
and queens

and shafts

inside
a pyramid.

The sides
of a pyramid

to build

in the pyramids
of Egypt.

There are
chambers

has

at the top.

Spots and Stripes

Read the story about different sharks.
If you find a new word, look at the words
around it to help work out the meaning.

There are 400 kinds of sharks in the world's oceans.
Many sharks have spots and stripes on their skin.
Some sharks have whirls and patterns instead of spots
and stripes. The marks on a shark's skin help it to hide
safely among the rocks or on the seafloor.

1 Draw a line to match the sentence to the shark name.

I have long yellow stripes
along my back.   leopard shark

I have white whirls and
patterns along my back.   silvertip

I have large black stripes
across my back.   carpetshark

hornshark

zebra shark

2 Read the story for clues to the meaning
of these words. Circle the correct answer.

(a) What is another word for "whirls"?

| swirls | hair | spines |

(b) What is the meaning of "seafloor"?

| bottom of the sea | top of the sea | waves |

3 Unscramble these letters to make words from the story.

(a) snik ....

(b) khars ....

(c) socnea ....

(d) pertiss ....

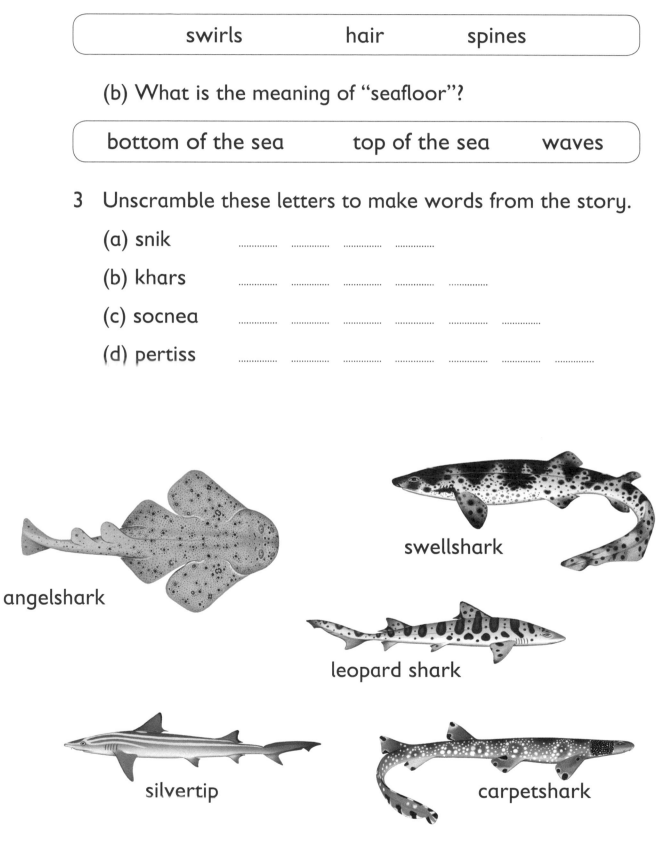

angelshark

swellshark

leopard shark

silvertip

carpetshark

Dinosaur Puzzles

Learn about how dinosaur bones are put together. Use a dictionary to find the meaning of new words. Try the word puzzles, too.

Dinosaurs were reptiles that lived long ago. Almost everything we know about them comes from studying their bones and tracks. Fossil bones are often jumbled up. People fit the bones together to make a complete skeleton. It is like doing a difficult jigsaw puzzle.

1 Look closely at the picture and then at the words in the box. Choose six things that you think you would need to make a dinosaur toolkit.

glue	goggles	pen	mask
welding torch	cup	gloves	safety shoes
clock	toothbrush	ladder	chocolate

(a) .... (b) ....

(c) .... (d) ....

(e) .... (f) ....

2   Read the sentences and answer Yes (Y) or No (N).

(a) We know a lot about dinosaurs
    by studying their bones.   ....

(b) It is easy to make a dinosaur skeleton.   ....

(c) Dinosaurs are still alive today.   ....

(d) Fossil bones are often mixed up.   ....

3   How many words of three letters or more
    can you make from this word?

d   i   n   o   s   a   u   r

....

....

....

....

4 = very good
6 = excellent

Tomb Painting

Let's find out about ancient Egypt. Complete the fun activities when you finish reading the story.

Pharaohs were the kings and queens of ancient Egypt. A pharaoh was buried in a tomb inside a pyramid. Artists painted the inside of a tomb with scenes from the owner's life. Some paintings show gods and animals. The artists used brightly colored paint made from ground rock.

1   Answer these questions about the story.

(a) What is a pharaoh?

....

(b) Where do we find the tomb of a pharaoh?

....

(c) In ancient Egypt, what was colored paint made from?

....

2   Look at the tomb-painting picture.
    Can you name an animal you can see?

....

3 Find the words in the story that rhyme with

(a) sock   ....

(b) beans   ....

(c) sings   ....

4 Spot the differences between these two pictures.
  Picture B has four differences.

....

....

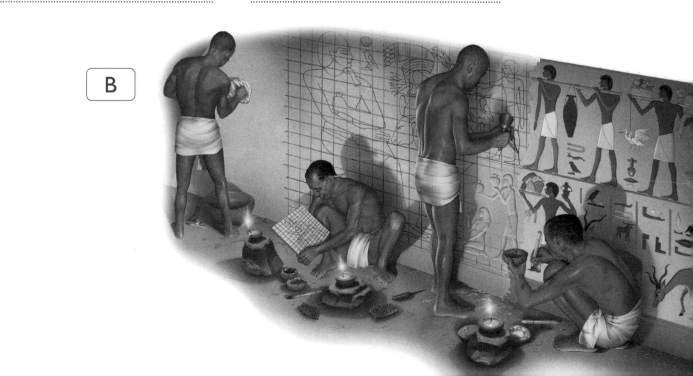

Underwater Treasure

Let's find out about underwater treasure. Try to sound out new words, then enjoy completing the fun activities.

Oceans are areas of water that make up a big part of our planet. Many wrecks lie on the seafloor. Divers explore them to find out more about how people lived long ago. Sometimes, divers find treasures under the sea. These are gathered carefully so they are not broken.

1   Are these sentences True or False?
    Write your answer in the space provided.

    (a) Oceans make up a small part of our planet. ....

    (b) Treasure can be found under the sea. ....

    (c) Scary fish always guard treasure under the sea. ....

What do divers carry on their back?

2 Here are some words from the story. Draw a line from each word to the word with the opposite meaning.

on	ignore
explore	small
more	hide
big	few
under	carelessly
find	less
carefully	over
many	off

3 Work through the maze to help the diver find the underwater treasure.

Asian Bears

What do you know about Asian bears?
Read the story to find out more and then try
the word puzzles, too.

Asian black bears and sloth bears live in Asia.
Both bears have a pointy face and a patch of white fur
on their chest. The Asian black bear is sometimes called
the moon bear because its white fur looks like part of
the Moon. Sloth bears have long, shaggy fur.

Asian black bear

1 Color the stars that fit the description of the bear.

	Asian black bear	Sloth bear
(a) I am also known as the moon bear.	☆	☆
(b) I live in Asia.	☆	☆
(c) I have long, shaggy fur.	☆	☆
(d) I have white fur like the Moon.	☆	☆
(e) I have a patch of white fur on my chest.	☆	☆
(f) I have a pointy nose.	☆	☆

Use the pictures to answer the next questions.

	Asian black bear	Sloth bear
(g) I have white fur on my face.	☆	☆
(h) I am standing up straight.	☆	☆
(i) I am resting on a rock.	☆	☆

2 Choose the correct words from the box to finish the sentences.

> roar   growl   croak   grunt   hiss

(a) A bear can ....

(b) A lion can ....

(c) A snake can ....

(d) A pig can ....

(e) A frog can ....

☆ What is another name for an Asian black bear?

Sloth bear

Bashful Bats

Read the story about bashful bats. If you find a new word, look at the words around it to help work out the meaning.

Bats are the only mammals that fly. They sleep during the day and hunt for food at night. At night it is hard to see. Bats send out high note sounds that bounce back off things around them. The echo helps them work out where things are.

1   Read the story. Match these sentence beginnings with the correct sentence ends.

At night it is hard	the day.
Bats sleep during	at night.
Bats hunt	that fly.
Bats are the only mammals	to see.

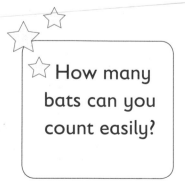 How many bats can you count easily?

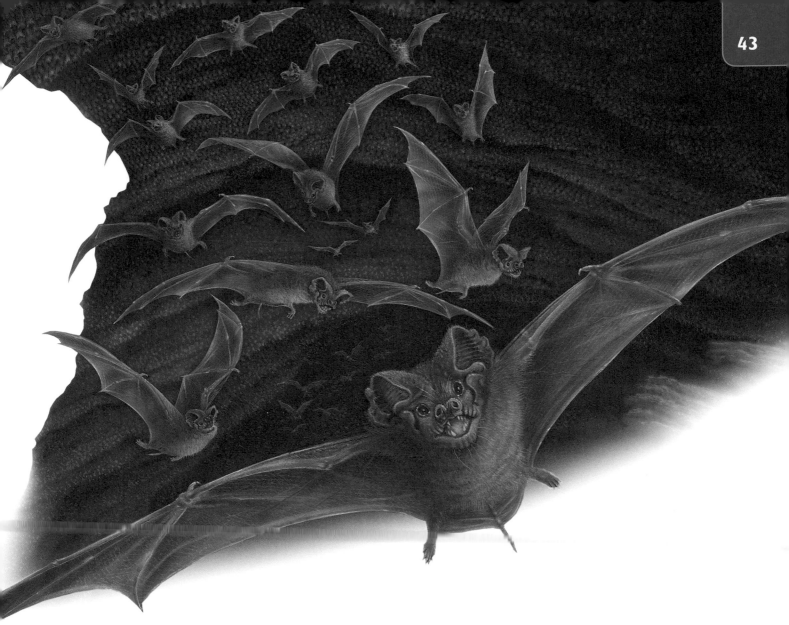

2 Remix these animal anagrams. One has been done for you.

Remix "tab" to make a word for a flying mammal.

Answer: bat

(a) Remix "tar" to make a word for an animal that looks like a mouse.

....

(b) Remix "god" to make a word for a pet that barks.

....

(c) Remix "low" to make a word for a bird of the night.

....

(d) Remix "act" to make a word for a pet that drinks milk.

....

Underwater Food Chain

Learn about the food chain under the sea, then have fun completing the activities. They will help you understand more about the world around you.

The ocean's food chain begins with very tiny creatures called plankton. It finishes with huge whales such as the orca. The plankton are eaten by small fish. The small fish are eaten by bigger fish. The bigger fish are eaten by seals and the seals are eaten by orcas.

1 Number these sentences from 1 to 4 to make a food chain.

.... The bigger fish are eaten by seals.

.... The plankton are eaten by small fish.

.... The seals are eaten by orcas.

.... The small fish are eaten by bigger fish.

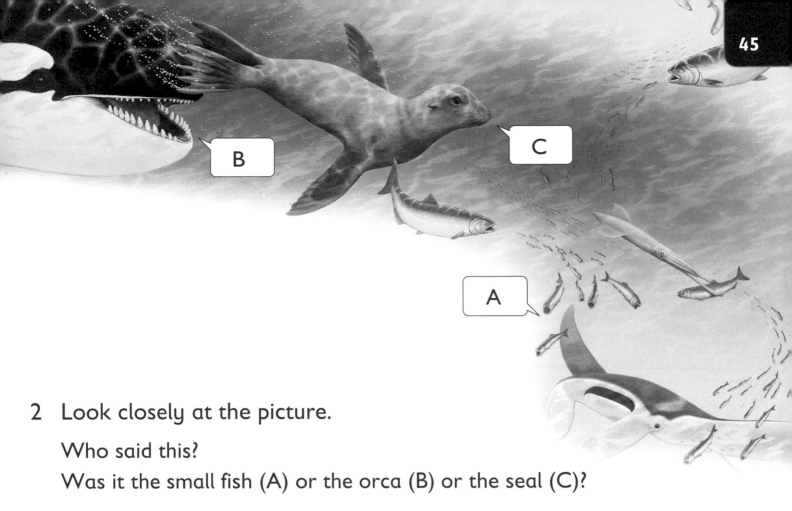

2 Look closely at the picture.

Who said this?

Was it the small fish (A) or the orca (B) or the seal (C)?

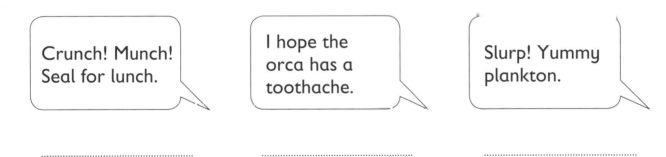

Crunch! Munch! Seal for lunch.

I hope the orca has a toothache.

Slurp! Yummy plankton.

....

3 Circle the odd one out.

(a) | ocean | sand | sea | water |

(b) | seaweed | orca | fish | seal |

(c) | small | tiny | mouse | little |

(d) | wash | eat | crunch | munch |

Our Brain

What do you know about our brain? Read the story. If you find a new word, look at the words around it to help work out the meaning.

Our body is amazing. Every part has its own job to do. Our brain tells our body what to do. There are special parts in the brain for our different senses, such as sight and taste. Our brain works all the time, even when we are asleep.

1   Look at the picture. Color the correct star as you find the pictures that show where these are in the brain.

☆ touch

☆ sleep

☆ sight

☆ smell

☆ taste

☆ hearing

2   Circle the words in the box that rhyme with "brain."

drain	crane	grain	shone
crumb	rain	lane	mind

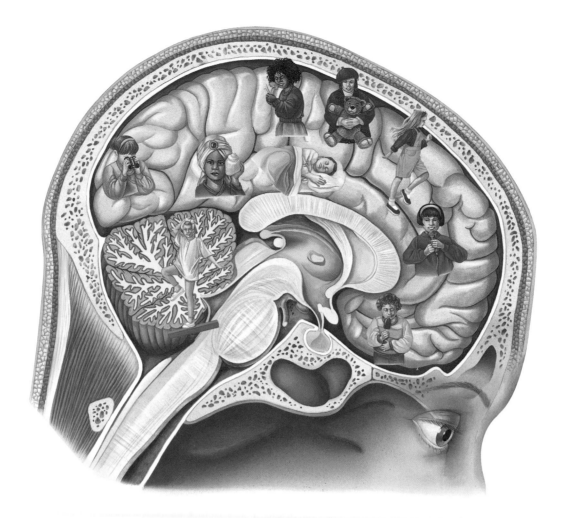

3   Look at the picture. Color in the stars that show you which part of the brain is being used.

	Front	Middle	Back
speech	☆	☆	☆
balance	☆	☆	☆
hearing	☆	☆	☆
smell	☆	☆	☆
taste	☆	☆	☆
sight	☆	☆	☆
movement	☆	☆	☆
touch	☆	☆	☆
sleep	☆	☆	☆

Helpful Huskies

What do you know about dogs that help us?
Here is a story about dogs called huskies. Read
the story, then enjoy completing the activities.

There are hundreds of different breeds of dogs.
Huskies are strong dogs with thick coats. They have a
white face, and ears shaped like triangles. Huskies help
people by pulling loads across the snow. They often
work in teams. Huskies work in Alaska as sled dogs.

1   Color in the star next to the correct answer.

(a) Huskies work as sled dogs in ....
     ☆ Alaska   ☆ Africa   ☆ Australia

(b) Huskies have ears shaped like ....
     ☆ sleds   ☆ triangles   ☆ squares

(c) The tail of a husky is ....
     ☆ straight   ☆ short   ☆ curly

(d) How does a thick coat help a husky to live?
     ☆ keeps out fleas   ☆ keeps out the cold
     ☆ helps it to swim

2   How do huskies help people?

....

3 Use the box of words to fill in the puzzle with the names of these different breeds of dog.

CHIHUAHUA

MASTIFF

PEKINESE

SAMOYED

WOLFHOUND

				H				
				U				
				S				
				K				
				Y				

What is this team of huskies pulling?

The Clean Machine

Do you know how a vacuum cleaner works? Use a dictionary to find the meaning of new words. Try the word puzzles, too.

How do machines and tools work? A vacuum cleaner is a machine that helps us to clean our homes. It has a motor that drives a spinning fan. A powerful flow of air sucks up dirt and dust. This sucks air and dust through the long hose. Then it traps the dust inside a dust bag.

1   Read the story for clues to the meaning of these words. Circle the correct answer.

(a) What is another word for "powerful"?

weak	strong	wet

(b) What is another word for "spinning"?

turning	jumping	skipping

(c) What is another word for "hose"?

pipe	switch	clean cloth

2 Number these sentences in the correct order.

.... Dust and air travels through the long hose.

.... The motor drives a spinning fan.

.... Dust is trapped in the dust bag.

.... A powerful flow of air sucks up dust.

3 What clean machine am I?

My first letter is in "bat" but not in "hat."

My second letter is in "run" but not in "fun."

My third letter is in "cot" but not in "cut."

My fourth letter is in "lot" but not in "let."

My last letter is in "gem" but not in "gel."

I am a ....

4 Draw me in the box below.

Kinds of Rocks

Let's find out about different kinds of rocks. When you have finished reading the story, complete the fun activities.

Rocks are all around us and we use them every day. People collect rock and use it to make buildings and machines. Most modern buildings are made from steel, concrete, and glass. All these come from rock. Rocks come in different shapes, sizes, and colors.

1   Look closely at the pictures and read their labels to answer these questions.

(a) I am a blue rock.

My name is ....

(b) I am a pink rock.

My name is ....

(c) I am made of smaller stones stuck together.

My name is ....

(d) I am a black, shiny rock.

My name is ....

2 Color in the star next to the correct answers.

People collect and use rocks for ....

☆ buildings ☆ food ☆ machines

☆ glass windows ☆ steel fences ☆ books

3 Look around you. List two things you can see made from rock.

....

....

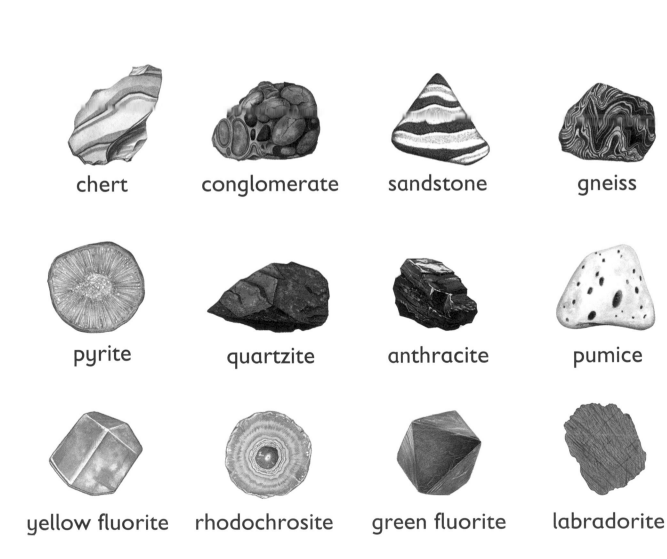

chert   conglomerate   sandstone   gneiss

pyrite   quartzite   anthracite   pumice

yellow fluorite   rhodochrosite   green fluorite   labradorite

Life in the Spinifex

Read the story about life in the spinifex.
If you find a new word, look at the words
around it to help work out the meaning.

Deserts are places where there is little or no rain.
They are very hot during the day and very cold at night.
Spinifex grass grows in Australian deserts. Its leaves are
stiff and pointy. Birds, snakes, lizards, insects, and tiny
rodent or rat-like animals live in the spinifex grass.

1 Look at the picture and the key next to it.
   Color in the correct star as you find each animal.

   ☆ ningaui

   ☆ crimson chat

   ☆ cockroach

   ☆ desert skink

   ☆ gecko

   ☆ legless lizard

2   Look closely at the picture and then answer
these questions.

(a) Which animal is eating an insect?

....

(b) Name the animal with no legs.

....

(c) How many cockroaches did you find?

....

(d) Name the animal that is a rodent.

....

(e) What is spinifex?

....

Key

ningaui

gecko

cockroach

crimson chat

desert skink

legless lizard

Heavenly Colors

Let's learn about why the rainbow has colors. Then complete the activities. They will help you understand more about the weather.

Rainbows come out when sunlight shines through raindrops. The water drops split up the light into different colors. Sunlight looks white, but it is really made up of many different colors. Raindrops also scatter sunlight into different directions. We see the shape of a rainbow as an arch.

1 Match these jigsaw parts to make sentences.
   Color the parts that make one sentence the same color.

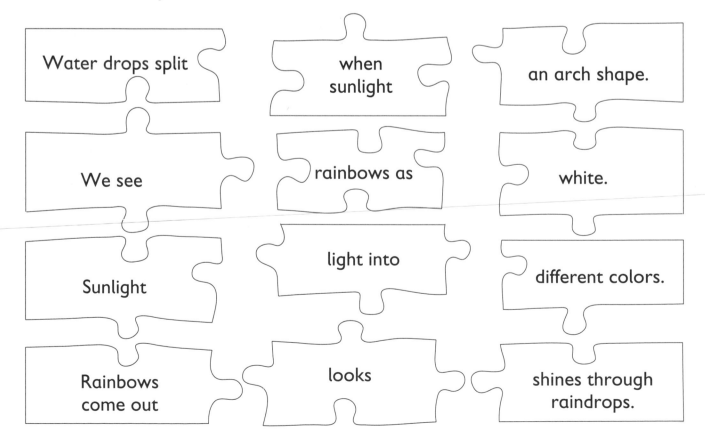

Water drops split | when sunlight | an arch shape.

We see | rainbows as | white.

Sunlight | light into | different colors.

Rainbows come out | looks | shines through raindrops.

Colored Arch

2 Use the key to write the colors of the rainbow in the correct order. Start with red.

....

....

....

....

....

....

....

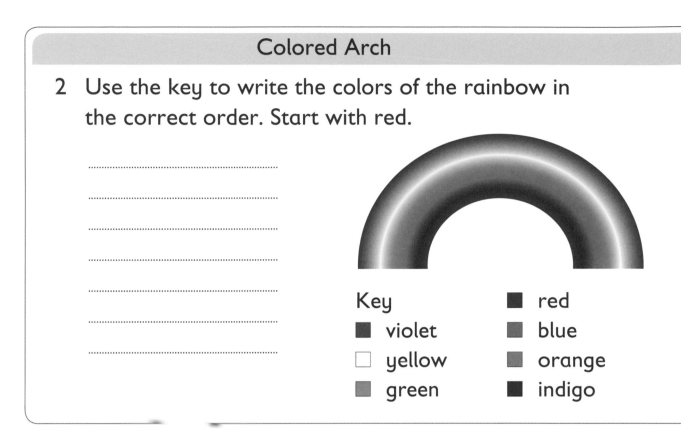

Key   ■ red

■ violet   ■ blue

☐ yellow   ■ orange

■ green   ■ indigo

3 The word "rainbow" is a compound word.
It is made up of "rain" + "bow."
Split up each of these compound words.

(a) sunlight   = ...   + ...

(b) birthday   = ...   + ...

(c) sunflower   = ...   + ...

(d) jigsaw   = ...   + ...

Super Swingers

Read the story about monkeys in the jungle. Try to sound out new words, then enjoy completing the activities.

Monkeys live in jungles in Africa, Asia, and America. South American spider monkeys use their tail to swing from tree to tree. These monkeys eat fruit that they pick from the trees. The baby spider monkey wraps its tail around its mother. It does not want to fall off.

1   Read the story, look at the picture, then say whether these sentences are True or False. Color in the star next to the correct answer.

(a) Monkeys live in the North Pole.
☆ True   ☆ False

(b) The spider monkey eats fruit.
☆ True   ☆ False

(c) Monkeys use their arms to swing.
☆ True   ☆ False

(d) Spider monkeys have a long tail.
☆ True   ☆ False

(e) Spider monkeys live only on the ground.
☆ True   ☆ False

2 Read the sentences below and decide whether to use "it's" or "its." Circle the correct one. (Remember that it's = it is)

(a) The baby spider monkey wraps ...its / it's... tail around ...its / it's... mother.

(b) ...Its / It's... very hot and warm in the jungle.

(c) A baby monkey knows that with ...its / it's... mother ...its / it's... always safe.

3 Fill in the no-clues crossword with the words from the list below.

MONKEY

SPIDER

JUNGLE

TAIL

SWING

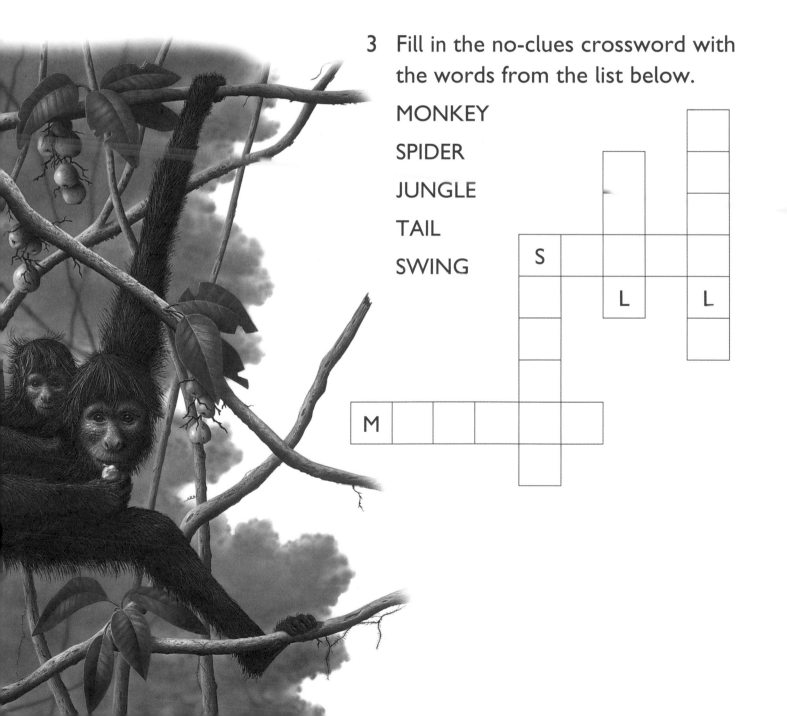

In the Trees

What do you know about animals that live in the jungle? Use a dictionary to find the meaning of new words. Try the word puzzles, too.

Jungles are warm and wet forests. Many jungle animals live high up in the trees. They howl, chirp, call, and sing as they move through the branches. Many birds with bright colors live in the jungles of South America.

1 Who am I? Look at the picture and color in the correct star when you find me.

☆ I swing from tree to tree. I am a monkey.

☆ We are red and blue parrots. We are macaws.

☆ I am a bird with a long colorful tail. I am a quetzal.

2 What is it? Write the correct answer.

| frog | spider | snake | monkey |

(a) It spins a web to catch flies. ....

(b) It uses its arms and tail to move through the trees. ....

(c) It glides along the ground. ....

(d) It is a colorful amphibian and croaks loudly. ....

3 You can play this activity with a friend. You use the words "In the jungle I saw…" One player starts by naming a creature they saw in the jungle. Take it in turns to add a new creature. Each player has to say all the animals named as well as adding a new one.

For example:

Player 1: In the jungle I saw a tiger.
Player 2: In the jungle I saw a tiger and a monkey.
Player 1: In the jungle I saw a tiger, a monkey, and a snake. and so on …

If you forget one of the creatures – miss a turn!

The Roman Army

Let's find out about the army of ancient Roman times. Complete the fun activities when you finish reading the story.

Today, Rome is the capital city of Italy. Two thousand years ago, Rome ruled many parts of the world. These parts were called the Roman Empire. A very large army of soldiers protected the Roman Empire. When soldiers moved around, they carried all their tools and weapons, and enough food for three days.

1   Spot the differences between these two pictures. Picture B has six differences.

....

....

....

....

....

....

A

2   Imagine you are a Roman soldier.
    You can carry only eight items of food to live on
    for three days. List them here. Remember you must
    carry the food all day (until you eat it, of course!).

    ....

    ....

    ....

    ....

3   Color in the star next to the correct answer.

    (a) Two thousand years ago, parts of the world were called
        ☆ the kingdom of Rome   ☆ Rome
        ☆ the Roman Empire

    (b) Today, Rome is the capital of
        ☆ France   ☆ Italy   ☆ Spain

    (c) The Roman Empire was protected by
        ☆ a large army   ☆ a strong wall
        ☆ a large airforce

    B

Eating Food

Read the story about eating food. If you find a new word, look at the words around it to help work out the meaning.

Gas is the fuel for a car. Food is the fuel for our body. We chew food and swallow it. Then, our digestive system turns it into small bits that our body can use. Digested food gives us energy to move. It builds strong bones and muscles.

1 Finish these sentences.

(a) Gas is the fuel for ....

(b) We chew food and ....

(c) The digestive system turns food into

....

(d) Digested food builds ....

2 Unscramble these letters to make words from the story.

(a) lfue ....

(b) wwllaos ....

(c) sebon ....

(d) doof ....

3 Look closely at the picture. The food lump is going down the food pipe. Where will it go next?
Color in the star next to the correct answer.

☆ small intestine   ☆ large intestine   ☆ stomach

4 Here's a list of types of food. Put a circle around the ones you like and cross out the ones you don't like.

milk	hamburgers	cheese
chocolate	sandwiches	pizza
broccoli	ice cream	cabbage
apples	tomatoes	carrots
beef	bananas	yogurt

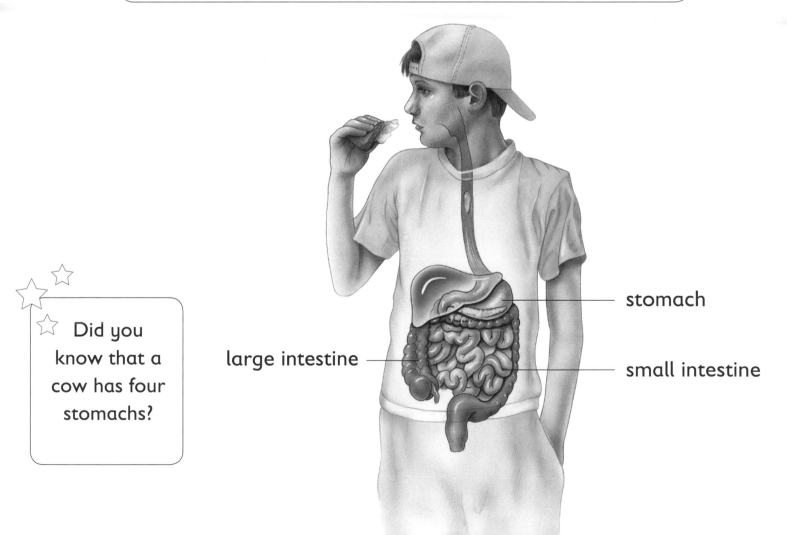

☆
☆
☆ Did you know that a cow has four stomachs?

large intestine

stomach

small intestine

Chapters of History

Here is a list of chapters for the story about the Trojan Horse. Read it, then complete the activities.

The Trojan Horse is a story of adventure in ancient Greece. The Contents page below lists the chapters of a book that tells the story of the Trojan Horse. The page numbers tell you where to find that part of the story.

Contents

Ancient Greece	4
At the Palace	6
Helen Runs Away	8
War Breaks Out	10
City of Troy	12
Achilles and Hector	14
Achilles Dies	16
Building the Horse	18
Through the Gates	20
The Greeks Attack	22
Greek Victory	24
Ruins of Troy	26
Mask of Agamemnon	28
Quiz	30
Glossary	31

Use the Contents page to answer the following questions.

1 Who ran away from the palace?

....

2 Which page number starts the chapter "Building the Horse"?

....

3 Color in the star next to the correct answer.

(a) Which happened first?
☆ Building the Horse   ☆ Greek Victory   ☆ War Breaks Out

(b) How many chapters of the story are there?
☆ 16 chapters   ☆ 15 chapters   ☆ 13 chapters

(c) Guess the meaning of the word "glossary"?
☆ a list of word meanings   ☆ a large bird
☆ a sort of sword

4 Use the letters of the word "TROY" to fill in this sudoku. Every column, row, and mini-grid must contain the letters of this word.

Y			O
		Y	
		T	
T	R		Y

Answers

4–5

1. (a) tails and fins
   (b) fish and seals
   (c) the swimmer's arms and flippers
2. (a) sharp
   (b) scary
   (c) large
   (d) powerful
3. Crossword
4. shark

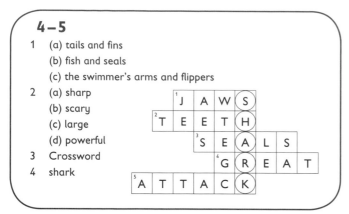

6–7

1. (a) False
   (b) True
   (c) True
   (d) False
   (e) True
2. Possible answers include:
   to keep the sand out of their face; to stop sunburn
3. The Sahara Desert is very sandy.

8–9

1. (a) search dog
   (b) Great Dane
   (c) cattle dog
   (d) Great Dane
   (e) search dog
   (f) cattle dog
2. (a) frog   (b) log
   (c) fog   (d) jog
3. Maze

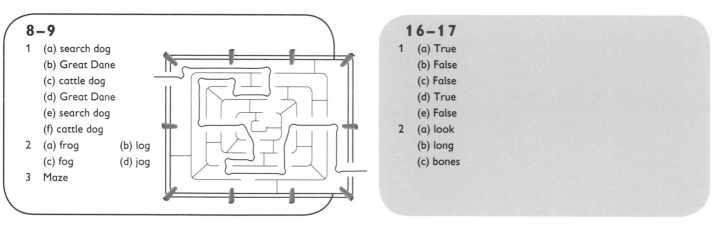

10–11

1. (a) Troy   (b) inside the wooden horse   (c) the city wall
2. 3 The wooden horse was left outside the city of Troy.
   2 Greek soldiers hid in the wooden horse.
   5 The Greek soldiers jumped out of the horse.
   4 The Trojans took the wooden horse inside the city.
   1 Odysseus built a wooden horse.
3.
   crafty — empty
   gift — clever
   wooden — made of wood
   hollow — very big
   huge — present

12–13

1. 2 The row of tiny pins moves.
   3 The row of pins lines up straight.
   1 The key goes into the lock.
   4 The lock opens.
2. see, she, be, sea, free
3. (a) lock and key   (b) salt and pepper
   (c) cup and saucer   (d) shoes and socks
   (e) knife and fork   (f) table and chair
4. Maze = C

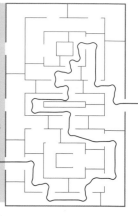

14–15

1. (a) the Plains
   (b) horses
   (c) meat and clothing
2. (a) fat
   (b) lamps
   (c) meat
   (d) horses
3. Help! Get out of my way! C
   I have lots of arrows to help me hunt. B
   My spear is sharp and my horse is fast. A

16–17

1. (a) True
   (b) False
   (c) False
   (d) True
   (e) False
2. (a) look
   (b) long
   (c) bones

18–19

1. (a) rain gauge
   (b) thermometer
   (c) to protect it from the sun
3. (a) The boy and girl are wearing cold-weather clothes.
   (b) The leaves have fallen off the tree.
4. Word search

20–21

1 (a) True
  (b) True
  (c) False
2 (a) wine, food
  (b) Vesta
  (c) keeping a fire burning
3 Word search

```
            V B K A J
            V M A T E
            E R T H E
            S A S N Z A
        B N T S N A E P H
      D C I A G A E U O E
      M P K V Z C U L R R
    C J H E R M E S O E R
    C P Q C G N B M L A A
    N M R Y D Z P S O E E
    A P H R O D I T E Q O Y R
    P O S E I D O N H Z Y Q X
```

22–23

1 (a) True
  (b) False
  (c) False
  (d) True
2 emperor penguin A
  Magellanic penguin C
  chinstrap penguin B
3 Crossword

```
                    P
                    E                W O R L D
                    N                A
                    G                T
                    U                E
            F L I P P E R S
                    N                W
                                     I
                                     M
```

24–25

1 (a) True
  (b) False
  (c) False
  (d) True
2 (a) food
  (b) long
  (c) smoke
  (d) top
  (e) skins

3 Sudoku

```
I  S  K  N
K  N  S  I
S  I  N  K
N  K  I  S
```

Star box: cooking

26–27

1 (a) It turns into stone as time passes.
  (b) plants, insects, fish
2 Usually, only the hard bony parts of animals are strong enough to make fossils.
3 Crossword
4 fossil

```
        L E A F
          B O N E S
            S T O N E
  I M P R E S S I O N
            I N S E C T S
          P L A N T S
```

28–29

1 (a) tearing, digging, climbing
  (b) untidy
  (c) forests
2 (a) True
  (b) True
  (c) False
3 Word search

```
                A
              B   S S
            G R P O I
          B R O E L P A
        C L I W C S O U N
      Z U A Z N U P L A U D
        B C Z U P C T A R N
          K L Y P C L H A
            Y Q L E P
              W E D
                P
                D
```

30–31

1 pyramid

```
            B Y
          S O N
        K N O W
      E I G H T
    B I L L E D
```

2 A pyramid has sides shaped like triangles.
  Did it take a long time to build a pyramid?
  Dead kings and queens are buried in the pyramids of Egypt.
  The sides of a pyramid meet at the top.
  There are chambers and shafts inside a pyramid.

32–33

1 I have long yellow stripes along my back. → carpetshark
  I have white whirls and patterns along my back. → leopard shark
  I have large black stripes across my back. → silvertip
2 (a) swirls
  (b) bottom of the sea
3 (a) skin   (b) shark
  (c) oceans (d) stripes

34–35

1 Possible answers include:
  glue, goggles, mask, gloves, welding torch, safety shoes, ladder
2 (a) Y   (b) N
  (c) N   (d) Y
3 Possible answers include:
  (a) Words with three letters: aid, air, and, din, duo, nor, oar, our, sad, sin, sir, sod, son, sun, ran, rid, rod, run, urn

3 continued
  (b) Words with four letters: arid, iron, ours, rain, rind, road, ruin, runs, said, soda, sour, undo
  (c) Words with five letters: adorn, drain, rains, round, ruins, sound
  (d) Words with six letters: around, ordain, radius, unsaid

Answers continued

36–37

1 (a) a king or queen of ancient Egypt
   (b) inside a pyramid   (c) rock
2 Possible answers include: deer, bird, snake, antelope
3 (a) rock
   (b) scenes, queens
   (c) kings
4 eye missing from wall
   tool missing from floor
   extra antler on deer
   red vase

38–39

1 (a) False   (b) True   (c) False
2 on   ignore
   explore   small
   more   hide
   big   few
   under   carelessly
   find   less
   carefully   over
   many   off
3 Maze
Star box: an air tank

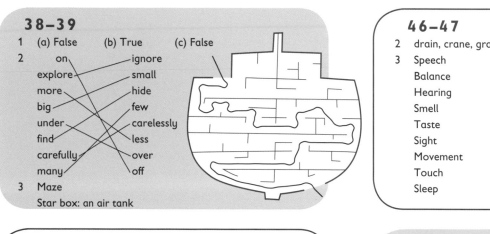

40–41

1 (a) Asian black bear
   (b) Asian black bear and sloth bear
   (c) sloth bear
   (d) Asian black bear
   (e) Asian black bear and sloth bear
   (f) Asian black bear and sloth bear
   (g) sloth bear
   (h) Asian black bear
   (i) sloth bear

2 (a) growl
   (b) roar
   (c) hiss
   (d) grunt
   (e) croak
Star box: moon bear

42–43

1 At night it is hard   the day.
   Bats sleep during   at night.
   Bats hunt   that fly.
   Bats are the only mammals   to see.
2 (a) rat
   (b) dog
   (c) owl
   (d) cat
Star box: 15

44–45

1 3 The bigger fish are eaten by seals.
   1 The plankton are eaten by small fish.
   4 The seals are eaten by orcas.
   2 The small fish are eaten by bigger fish.
2 Crunch! Munch! Seal for lunch. B
   I hope the orca has a toothache. C
   Slurp! Yummy plankton. A
3 (a) sand   (b) seaweed
   (c) mouse   (d) wash

46–47

2 drain, crane, grain, rain, lane
3 Speech   Front
   Balance   Back
   Hearing   Back
   Smell   Middle
   Taste   Front
   Sight   Back
   Movement   Front
   Touch   Middle
   Sleep   Middle

48–49

1 (a) Alaska
   (b) triangles
   (c) curly
   (d) keeps out the cold
2 They pull loads across the snow.
3 Crossword
Star box: a sled

W	O	L	F	H	O	U	N	D	
C	H	I	H	U	A	H	U	A	
		M	A	S	T	I	F	F	
		P	E	K	I	N	E	S	E
		S	A	M	O	Y	E	D	

50–51

1 (a) strong
   (b) turning
   (c) pipe
2 3 Dust and air travels through the long hose.
   1 The motor drives a spinning fan.
   4 Dust is trapped in the dust bag.
   2 A powerful flow of air sucks up dust.
3 broom

52–53
1 (a) labradorite
   (b) rhodochrosite
   (c) conglomerate
   (d) anthracite
2 buildings, machines, glass windows, steel fences

60–61
2 (a) spider
   (b) monkey
   (c) snake
   (d) frog

54–55
2 (a) ningaui
   (b) legless lizard
   (c) two
   (d) ningaui
   (e) grass

62–63
1 horn missing
   ornament missing from belt
   hand at top of pole turned opposite way
   plume missing from helmet
   metal disk is missing from the pole
   belt decoration different color
3 (a) the Roman Empire
   (b) Italy
   (c) a large army

56–57
1 Water drops split light into different colors.
   We see rainbows as an arch shape.
   Sunlight looks white.
   Rainbows come out when sunlight shines through raindrops.
2 red, orange, yellow, green, blue, indigo, violet
3 (a) sun + light
   (b) birth + day
   (c) sun + flower
   (d) jig + saw

64–65
1 (a) a car
   (b) swallow it
   (c) small bits
   (d) strong bones and muscles
2 (a) fuel
   (b) swallow
   (c) bones
   (d) food
3 stomach

58–59
1 (a) False
   (b) True
   (c) True
   (d) True
   (e) False
2 (a) its, its
   (b) It's
   (c) its, it's
3 Crossword

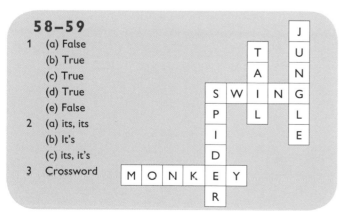

66–67
1 Helen
2 page 18
3 (a) War Breaks Out
   (b) 13 chapters
   (c) a list of word meanings
4 Sudoku

Conceived and produced by
Weldon Owen Pty Ltd
59–61 Victoria Street, McMahons Point
Sydney NSW 2060, Australia

Copyright © 2009 Weldon Owen Pty Ltd

BONNIER BOOKS
Group Publisher John Owen

WELDON OWEN PTY LTD
Chief Executive Officer Sheena Coupe
Creative Director Sue Burk
Associate Publisher Helen Bateman
Senior Vice President, International Sales Stuart Laurence
Vice President Sales: United States and Canada Amy Kaneko
Vice President Sales: Asia and Latin America Dawn Low
Administration Manager, International Sales Kristine Ravn
Publishing Coordinator Gina Belle

Concept Design Kathryn Morgan
Designer Juliana Titin
Art Manager Trucie Henderson

Production Manager Todd Rechner
Production Coordinators Lisa Conway, Mike Crowton

Illustration and Photo Credits
Cover Richard Hook
4-5 Christer Eriksson, 6-7 Chris Forsey, 8tl Ray
Grinaway, 8bc Guy Troughton, 9 Tom Connell/The Art
Agency, 11 Chris Forsey, 13 iStock, 14-15 Connell Lee,
17 Ray Grinaway, 18-19 Lorraine Hannay, 20-21 Kenn
Backhaus, 23 David Kirshner, 25 Richard Hook, 26 Peter
Schouten, 27 Anne Bowman, 29 David Kirshner,
31 Malcolm Godwin/Moonrunner Design, 32 Ray
Grinaway, 35 Marco Sparaciari, 37t and 37b Darren
Pattenden, 38 and 39 Kevin Stead, 40 and 41 David
Kirshner, 43 John Mac, 45 Rod Scott, 47 Susanna Addario,
48-49 David Kirshner, 51 Rod Westblade, 53 Ray
Grinaway, 55 David Kirshner, 57 iStock, 58-59 Christer
Eriksson, 61 John Mac, 62-63 Ray Grinaway,
65 Peg Gerrity, 67 Peter Bull Art Studio

This edition created exclusively for Barnes & Noble, Inc under
ISBN: 978-1-4114-2794-5

Printed in Singapore by Craft Print International Ltd

A WELDON OWEN PRODUCTION